Bob Fraser —
Director & Founder of

Michael and hi⟩
marketplace Christianit⟩
and have witnessed his authentic lifestyle and passion for Jesus first hand. While the majority of Christians struggle with how to incorporate faith into their workplace, a genuine expression of belief is the everyday overflow in Michael's life. Every time I hear stories from Michael, it shatters the myth that faith and the workplace don't mix.

This book gives readers a glimpse into the Sermon on the Mount lifestyle for the average marketplace person, and gives a picture of what is looks like to live a lifestyle that testifies of the living God. The life Michael lives is a twofold expression of excellence: an outward expression of excellence that has resulted in Michael being "the best worker and employee," and a secondary expression of an excellent heart fully devoted to God.

What many people know about Michael is his ministry and his work ethic. What few people know about, is his relationship with God. Whenever I spend time with Michael, I leave with an ache to know God more. His intimacy with God is real and tangible, and a great inspiration to me!

Michael's story is one that I often tell believers to encourage them to experience Christ while on their 9 to 5 jobs. It's with great pleasure that I can now recommend his book, and encourage you to learn how to represent Christ in your workplace. For several years, Michael has been a speaker, panelist, and minister at our marketplace events, through Joseph International. His testimony encourages others to discover the face of Jesus in every area of life: from the prayer room to the coffee shop.

Get yourself a cup of coffee, sit back, and enjoy the read!

LATTES,
MOCHAS
AND
JESUS

How I Met Jesus in a Coffee Shop

By

Michael Stephens

CONTENTS

INTRODUCTION
By Jeff Page

When my wife and I moved to Kansas City in the summer of 2006, we came with a number of fears. We had lived in Memphis for ten years, and were curious to see what this new place would hold for us. My wife would be going to a ministry school for the first time, starting a new journey in her mid-30s. I had just finished seminary a few years prior, but had left a church job and decided to stay in the marketplace because that's where all of the "lost" people were. I was pretty arrogant about it, too. But in Kansas City, I was about to find out just how clueless I was about the ways of the Lord.

Even while working for a church, I picked up a part-time job at a coffeehouse after hearing of a pastor at Willow Creek in Illinois doing the same. I was fascinated by the prospect, and began what would ultimately become a career choice. I knew that in leaving my church position I would need to provide for my family, and began managing coffeehouses in the Memphis area.

When the Lord told us to leave and move to Kansas City, I was actually prepared to quit my job and join my wife in ministry, as she had done for me years prior. I spent a day praying and fasting about what God would have me do, and to my surprise, He told me to stay in the marketplace.

So I found myself two months later in Kansas City, transferred to another coffee house in the same company, trying to figure out what the Lord wanted me to do in this place.

This is where I met Michael Stephens.

My first impression of Michael was that he was a normal, quiet guy. We were actually a part of the same community of faith in Kansas City, so we had that in common already. However, I noticed that he didn't keep his ministry and his work separate. This was a new experience for me. I was used to being the only person in my job who followed Jesus, and watching someone not only follow Jesus, but act like it, was a shock.

As a manager, I didn't really know how to handle it. It was more than the knowledge that he was a part of a church community. And it was more than the occasional church-speak. He spoke about Jesus openly, and he worked with integrity. He didn't let his ministry get in the way of doing the job I was paying him to do.

As time passed, I began to see that Michael was connecting with customers in a way that I hadn't seen before. There were customers who actually came to the store just to see him. Let me clarify—almost every coffeehouse worth its weight has baristas who shine and whom the customers love. This was different. We had people from out of town who had never entered our store before asking for Michael because of what other customers had told them. There was one other unusual thing about when they would come to see him.

They would ask for "The Prophet."

As Michael shares his story, I want you to keep one thing clear in your mind: he's just a normal guy. I know this from working with him day after day, often at five in the morning before the rest of the world was awake. He was a great employee, but he wasn't always perfect, as he would attest. So what you're about to read in this book is not a story of "why Michael Stephens brings so much to the table." This is the story of God telling a guy "Do this," and that guy saying, "Okay."

Watching him follow Jesus through our cafe speaking to person after person, gave me the courage to do some of the things I felt the Lord telling me to do. When an employee was sick, we would get a couple of employees together and pray over her. We would spend time praying over the building, that the

Lord would be glorified. We would regularly have musicians come in and play music that glorified Jesus specifically.

If you're managing a business, particularly a retail business, and are reading this book, let me be up front about something. I got complaints sometimes, not just about Michael, but about some of the other things that were going on. However, I had to make a decision that I was still going to allow it to happen. That was one of the things that Michael's actions encouraged me to do. I knew that the Lord wanted these things to transpire, so I was going to create an atmosphere for it to happen, and I wasn't going to get credit.

And business never suffered, by the way. Never. In fact, it grew. Would my supervisors have been pleased about what was going down? Most certainly not. But whatever His reasons were, the Lord kept it hidden from them. He doesn't always.

Michael and I have both moved on from that place, and are each working for different companies now. However, during that season that we worked together, I watched God intersect the lives of countless people on a daily basis. I know that I was impacted just by watching it happen, and for those that were recipients of that gift, they are out there, somewhere. Like the Ethiopian eunuch after Philip shared with him the truth of Jesus, they went on their way, rejoicing.

LATTES,
MOCHAS
AND
JESUS

1
I'M NO PROPHET; I JUST WORK HERE

When I was younger, I read so many stories about the heroes of the Faith. I was inspired by the lives of the great revivalists such as George Whitfield, Charles Finny, Smith Wigglesworth, "Mother Etter," and John G. Lake. After reading stories about their major encounters with the Lord, encounters that left them changed and set apart, I longed for something similar. I thought that these kinds of experiences were necessary and pivotal to propelling someone into miracles, signs, wonders, the prophetic and ministry. However, to this day, I have never had one of these encounters.

In many ways I'm grateful for that. I have had a pretty normal life. I've developed a friendship with the Holy Spirit and a passion for knowing the Man

Christ Jesus. I grew up in a small town in southeast Texas and was raised primarily in a Baptist Church, although I did spend some time in a Church of Christ and in a Nazarene Church. The gifts of the Spirit were not spoken about much. Miracles were usually mentioned as something that happened in other countries and that, at best, were rare at best here in the United States.

Having moved from Texas, I spent my last two years of high school in Northwest Arkansas. We had a little group of zealous, rag-tag evangelists that prayed every morning at the flagpole. We witnessed at school. We were "bold for Christ." I was one of the main leaders in the group, and, though I loved prayer, worship, and preaching, I was passionately opposed to the gifts. In that opposition, I would even try to convince some of my friends that the gifts weren't in operation anymore.

But I had a secret.

My sophomore year of high school, while still living in the Houston area, I had a dream. In the dream, I was leading worship with a full band in a gym with gray floors, and there were a few hundred students there. After the first few songs, I preached for a few minutes on prayer.

When I woke up I thought, "Wow! That's a really cool dream!" While replaying the dream in my head, I felt the Lord say, "This is going to happen."

This was my first experience having a dream so vivid, detailed, and realistic. As grand as the dream may have been, I foresaw a problem to its fulfillment. I could only play three chords on the guitar and I was not a good public speaker. I had never really done either before. Regardless, I kept this dream close to my heart.

One night, a few months later, my youth pastor came and prayed for me. Just a few minutes before he prayed, I had felt the Lord saying that he was about to start preparing me for what I had dreamt months earlier. I did not tell my youth pastor anything about the dream or what I had felt like the Lord had said.

The day after my pastor prayed for me, he told me the youth group was going to be running the Church service on Sunday night, and he asked me if I would give the message. I'll never forget it. It was an incredibly short three minutes and twenty-three seconds! The youth attending, as well as the leaders, seemed to enjoy it, and over the next few months, I was asked to preach at church three or four times for Sunday night services.

Going into my senior year, I told a few people about the dream and that I believed we were going to have a worship concert in a basketball gym before my senior year was over. Sure enough, later that semester, the youth pastors in the area decided to get together and have an interdenominational worship concert in the high school basketball gym. A few weeks before the concert, the school threw out the old black tarps that had covered the gym floor and bought brand new gray ones.

About a half hour before it all started, one of the youth leaders came to me and asked me if I would speak for about ten minutes on the topic of prayer after the third worship song. I did. The dream God had given me came true.

There were a handful of experiences in my life, like the dream, that undeniably testified to a greater reality than what I was willing to admit was possible.

There were a few times when I actually prophesied over people, but I kept these times hidden in my heart. Two of the people I prophesied over have been my close friends now for almost 15 years. For whatever reason, I never spoke about these moments, and I was adamant that the gift of prophecy no longer existed. This attitude of doubt continued into college. Fortunately enough for me, my college roommate began to explore the spiritual gifts.

I told him to be careful and to not be deceived, but on the inside I was in turmoil. Maybe, just maybe, the gifts of the Spirit were not only real, but were meant to be walked in every day. While doctrine should never be created based on experience, I could not get around those events that testified to a higher reality which I could not argue against scripturally.

So, I decided to open myself up to the Lord and trust that he really was good. I believed that, as the Scripture says, if I asked the Lord for a fish he would not give me a snake, and if I asked him for bread he would not give me a stone. I began to ask the Lord to speak to me like he did in my youth.

I will never forget the first night that I began to hear him in prayer. I was praying for my friend Trent from John 14:12, where Jesus said that we would do greater works than He did. I was asking the Lord to stir up a spirit of prayer wherever Trent was. While I was praying for him, a picture flashed in my mind of my old cell phone ringing, with Trent's name appearing on the caller ID. About one minute later, the apartment phone rang, and it was Trent!

I asked him what was going on, and he told me that he was on his way to work on a school project, but was really feeling a stirring to get together and pray. He told me that Jesus' words about the "greater works" were on his heart! I was so excited! A few days later, I was in the car headed to work and was going to call a friend I hadn't spoken with in a few weeks. As I reached down to grab the phone, I felt the Lord say, "Don't call. She'll call you in ten minutes."

I looked at the clock and it was 10:26. At 10:36 the phone rang and it was her! I know it seems so small, but when you are hearing the voice of the Lord, what he has to say is never insignificant! There is nothing like knowing that he knows! I was beginning to get addicted to hearing the Lord. I found that I heard the Lord the most when I prayed for people.

That summer I would go to churches and stand in the back during worship. I would wait until someone stuck out to me and I would go up and pray for him or her. The first night I decided to go do this, I prayed for a young man. I prayed for some specific things regarding his relationship with his father, as well as some other details. I prayed, saying that he was a Joseph and the Lord was going to bless the work of his hands.

While I was praying for him, I saw in my mind the color and the design of his bed covers, where his bed was positioned in his bedroom, and where he sat when he read his Bible. However, I felt that I was not to share the details of what I had seen with him.

When I was done praying, he looked up at me and confirmed all that I had told him and asked how I knew his name was Joseph. I told him I didn't know anything and that I was simply telling him what the Lord had laid on my heart.

I went on to tell him that he would doubt what had happened later in the week, that friends would convince him it wasn't real. He said he didn't see how that was possible. I saw him the following week and he told me that his friends had convinced him that I had simply "read him," that what happened wasn't real. So I told him about what I saw in his bedroom. His eyes got super big and he said, "It is real!"

My roommate somehow ended up running into him years later and as they were talking my name came up. The guy still remembered the story and spoke of the impact it had on his life. Time went by and life happened. I continued to pray and prophesy over people here and there. I loved seeing the look on people's faces when they realized that Jesus really knew who they were.

After moving to Kansas City, I took a job with Starbucks, where I worked for about three years. After about 18 months, I was growing frustrated with being at work and not doing ministry. I felt that what I was called to do was ministry and anything else was second best.

One day while I was working, I thought, "If I am going to be here 40 hours a week, I might as well do something that I like." So, I looked around the store and saw two ladies sitting down having coffee. I walked over to them and said, "This may sound strange, but I asked the Lord what he thought about you and if you are interested I'd like to tell you." They both looked at me with what I call the puppy dog look (where someone turns their head to the side and looks at you funny). One of the ladies simply said, "Sure."

I began to prophesy over the first lady, then the second, and then over their relationship together and what the Lord was saying to them. At the end of it, I prayed for them. One of the ladies looked at me and said, "So, prophet, where did you come from?" I just laughed a little and said, "*I'm no prophet.* I just work here," and I went back to mopping the floor.

As I mopped, I thought about how great it would be if people came to Starbucks to hear from the Lord. I imagined some guy out there struggling with his faith, but instead of calling his pastor or minister, I pictured him getting into his car and going to Starbucks to get the word of the Lord. It seemed grand, but a little extreme. However, I was feeling the presence of the Lord at work, and I was hooked. I made up my mind. I would start prophesying over at least one table a day. I even had a little saying, "A table a day or the gift goes away."

Gideon

After a few months went by of me doing this every day at work, my confidence in the Lord's desire and ability to speak had grown exponentially. One day a young man came in and sat down at the same table the ladies had used. I walked over to him and said what I always said, "This may sound strange, but I asked the Lord what he thought about you, and if you are interested I'd like to tell you." He leaned back, crossed his arms, looked at me like he knew I was coming and said, "Okay... go."

I was a little thrown off by his response, but I started prophesying over him anyway. The Lord was bringing up things regarding his childhood, his battles, and, in particular, the struggle he had been having with his faith in the last five months. The whole time I was speaking, he was shaking his head and saying, "This is unbelievable."

Suddenly, as clear as I have ever heard the Lord, I heard, "Gideon!" I looked at the man and said, "The Lord says you're here like Gideon tonight, and he's not done with you yet." Immediately, he fell apart weeping. He was making a scene in the store. He went on to tell me that he had been struggling with his faith for the past five or six months. Earlier that day he had told his friend that he was "done" and that he did not believe in God anymore.

His friend told him, "Don't give up. Go to Starbucks. There is a guy there that I believe hears from the Lord, and if God is real, he will tell him to come talk to you." To this day, I am amazed at the faith of his friend. He didn't get my schedule, he didn't call to see if I was there, and he didn't try to talk to me and give me a heads up. He simply said, "If God is real, he will tell him to come talk to you."

The young man told me that five minutes before I walked up, he had sat down and said, "Lord, I'm here like Gideon tonight and this is my fleece." Wow! Right then and there the young man gave his heart back to the Lord. I saw him periodically over the next few months and every time I saw him, he was smiling and reading his Bible or another book about Christ.

Walk Through the Walls

On a separate occasion, there was a young man sitting down at a different table. I walked up to him and said what I always said, "This may sound strange, but I asked the Lord what he thought about you, and if you are interested I'd like to tell you." He seemed to be okay with it. But the next thing I did was out of the ordinary for me. I reached over and grabbed a chair to sit down, and I kind of made a big deal about it. I said more than once, "Is it okay if I sit down with you?" and, "I'm going to sit down with you for a minute."

In my head, I didn't understand why I was making such a big deal about it. I asked him what his name was. When he told me, it struck me in my heart. At the time, I had been looking at baby name books and I had seen his name recently, so I knew what it meant. I asked him, "Do you know what your name means?" He answered, "No." So, I told him what his name meant.

I didn't feel like I had much to tell him, so I said, "You know, if the Lord could walk through the walls of this coffee shop today and tell you one thing, I feel like he'd tell you that he loves you and likes you a lot." I prayed for him and I left discouraged.

The grandiose prophetic stories like my "Gideon" encounter were running through my head, and here I was telling this guy "God liked him." However, about twenty minutes later, he walked up and handed me a sheet of paper and said, "Please read this. Don't throw it away before reading it." I went in the back after he left and opened up what looked like a sheet of paper that had been torn out of a journal.

At the top of the page, he wrote a small thank you note that explained that he had just written the page in his journal a few minutes before I had walked up. It read something like this: "Lord, walk through the walls of the coffee shop today. Sit down with me. Tell me my name and that you love me and like me a lot."

I could not believe what I was reading. I thought that I had missed it. I was once again blown away by the kindness of the Lord.

Divine Appointment

It was a weekday afternoon, and the store was pretty empty when a woman came in to grab a quick drink. I overheard her talking to one of the other baristas as she was buying a teddy bear. All I heard was that the teddy bear was for her daughter, who was in the hospital. I'm not sure what came over me, but I was irritated. As I watched her walk back out to the car, where her husband and six month old were waiting, I knew that I could not let them drive away without praying for their daughter.

I quickly came out from behind the counter and ran after their car, waving them down as they were driving away. They rolled down the window, and I said, "I don't know what your religious background is and I don't care. I know this seems strange, but I heard you say your daughter is in the hospital, and it's not right. I'd like to pray for your daughter if that's okay." They looked at me surprised and explained to me that that their three year old was in the hospital. I began praying for their daughter and then proceeded to pray for them.

As I was praying for them, I said, "In two days you are going to have a divine appointment with a woman that you have never met, and two or three days after that she will set you up with the first doctor that will be able to fix your daughter." I blessed them and told them to have a good day. They seemed very thankful. However, I had no idea what I just prayed for. I especially had no idea what I meant when I said it would be "the first doctor" that would be able to fix their daughter.

Some months went by. On a busy weekday, as I was cleaning tables, a man stood up from his table to stop me and said, "Hi there. You're the face of the guy who prays for people right?"

I had never heard it put that way, but I said, "Sure."

He said, "I don't know how to adequately thank you." He probably said that phrase ten times over the next few minutes.

He went on: "About six months ago, my wife came in here to get a teddy bear for our daughter. We don't even live over here. We just decided to go for a drive, out of frustration, and somehow ended up at this coffee shop. We were going to head over to the hospital. You see our daughter had been on a feeding tube since birth. We had taken her to multiple doctors and specialist, but no one could fix her. We didn't know what to do. We had given up on everything, including the Lord, and were at our wit's end. When you prayed for our daughter and for us, we were so shocked and blessed that we gave our hearts back to the Lord right on the spot. Two days later, we had a divine appointment with a woman we had never met, and two days after that she set us up with the first doctor in three years that was able to fix our daughter."

Praise the Lord! I don't have all the answers for why the Lord heals one-way one day and another the next. All I know is that the girl couldn't eat on her own, that the prophetic word was spoken, and now she can eat on her own. Again and again… praise the Lord!

He Knows

Over the course of 18 months, I had the opportunity to pray for and prophesy over somewhere between 1,000 and 1,400 people (the best I can figure). Some days it was three or four, and some days it was 15. It just depended on how busy we were and how much I had to do as a shift manager. During that time, I started ending every interaction the same way. I would say, "The point of what just took place is not that a guy in Starbucks knew some things about you. The point is that there is a real man sitting on a real throne. His name is Jesus. And out of 6 billion people on the planet, he cared enough about you to tell a guy in Starbucks to come talk to you."

Over and over again, I saw the Lord reveal the secrets of people's hearts. Sometimes what he would say didn't even seem significant to me.

One night, I was on a break and trying to take a quick nap in my car. As I was trying to close my eyes, I heard the Lord say, "world religion."

I said, "I don't care." I was tired and grumpy.

He said, "She is studying world religion."

I sat up and looked around, and there was a girl reading a book in the window at the store. As I walked back in, I stopped and said, "Hey, I don't know if this means anything to you, but I was sitting in my car and the Lord told me that you were studying world religion."

She kind of grinned and held up her book and the cover read "Study of World Ethics and Religion." I did not know what to say, so I simply said, "I guess the Lord wanted you to know he knew what you were reading."

How incredible is God! He sits enthroned above the heavens, named the stars, put the galaxies in place, told the shore where to stop, formed the dry land and seas, has myriads of angels, and knew what that girl was reading in a coffee shop in Kansas City.

If you are ever struggling or asking the question "Does God know?" these stories should encourage your heart that he is aware and knows you.

Your destiny is not defined by the size of your checkbook or your vocation. Your job as CEO, personal trainer, mom, coach, photographer, janitor, business owner, manager, construction worker or whatever it may be, is not your meaningless lot in life in between Sundays and the occasional mission trip. Work is no longer a curse we live under (if we are in Christ), because every day that Jesus worked he redeemed the workplace and made it a place of encounter.

My desire as you read these stories is not that you are simply encouraged by them, but that they provoke you. I don't want you to challenge yourself or anything of the sorts. Challenges lose their punch and momentum, and you can always overcome a challenge. You can never overcome love. You can only go deeper and higher into him. My hope in your reading this is simple; that you would be provoked to love in every arena of life, that you would encounter him, and that others would encounter him through you.

2
THE BEST KIND OF LOVE

You were hand-picked. You were designed. You were a dream in God's heart that he could not wait to see come forth. It took him just six days to make all of the heavens and their glory; and, it took him an entire day to design one human being. He took his time. He wanted someone made in his image that had the full capacity to love and be encountered by him.

He did not want a robot programmed to obey. He did not want loyalty. He had the angels. He wanted someone with every capability not to love him to choose to love him. That is why Paul wrote that God chose or desired us in him... in love. Paul did not say, "He gave us no choice but to love him," or "He made us love him." It says he chose or desired us. God desires you and more importantly, has always desired you.

4just as He chose [desired] us in Him before the foundation of the world, that we should be holy and without blame before Him in love (Ephesians 1:4),

There has never been a point in eternal history when God did not know you and did not desire you. He designed your life in such a way that if you say yes to him, it will produce the greatest amount of love towards him in your heart. Jesus, the Father, and the Holy Spirit have been talking about you for eternity.

23I have been established from everlasting,
From the beginning, before there was ever an earth.
24When *there were* no depths I was brought forth,
When *there were* no fountains abounding with water.
25Before the mountains were settled,
Before the hills, I was brought forth;
26While as yet He had not made the earth or the fields,
Or the primal dust of the world.
27When He prepared the heavens, I *was* there,
When He drew a circle on the face of the deep,

²⁸When He established the clouds above,
When He strengthened the fountains of the deep,
²⁹When He assigned to the sea its limit,
So that the waters would not transgress His command,
When He marked out the foundations of the earth,
³⁰Then I was beside Him *as* a master craftsman;
And I was daily *His* delight,
Rejoicing always before Him,
³¹Rejoicing in His inhabited world,
And my delight *was* with the sons of men.

³²Now therefore, listen to me, *my* children,
For blessed *are those who* keep my ways.
(Proverbs 8:23-32)

In this Proverb, Jesus is describing what took place in Genesis 1, and more importantly what took place in his heart. There he was, before the Father, making all of creation, and it says that he was rejoicing in his inhabited world. His delight was with the sons of men. Jesus looked down the timeline of history, saw you in love with him, and began to rejoice before the Father.

One translation of the word "rejoice" is "to whirl about." Jesus danced over you!

The best part about this verse is that nowhere does it say, "But, he was really disappointed with their sin, and he was later grieved because he knew he would have to discipline them." No! He looked down the line of history, saw you in love (even if it feels weak) and said, "Dad, do you see them! I can't wait until they get here! I've got so much planned for them! You should see the way they love me!" Your sin does not surprise God!

> 16For "who has known the mind of the LORD that he may instruct Him?" But we have the mind of Christ (1 Corinthians 2:16).

This means God cannot be taught anything. He can't be taught anything because he already knows everything. If he already knows everything, it means that God has never had a new thought. Never once has someone told God something that caused him to say, "My goodness! I never thought of that. It never crossed my mind."

That doesn't mean that he is emotionless. He is an infinite God and has an endless capacity for emotions. That's why, after all of eternity, he was still rejoicing about you during the formation of creation. This means you have always been on God's mind and heart, and he has always been excited about you loving him back.

This is a difficult truth for most to grasp because we are so focused on our sin. We forget that, for all the time in eternity, God only has to judge our sin for however long we are alive. On average, that's around 80 to 100 years. That's a blink.

The reason that truth is hard to swallow is because we have spent most of our lives viewing God a certain way. We have viewed him as a taskmaster that requires a checklist of us that we can't complete.

We think that the story goes like this: Jesus felt bad for us and took the wrath of the mean Father, and the Holy Spirit came to help us not mess up quite as much and be our "get-out-of-Hell-free" card.

We must shift the way we view God viewing us. Jesus was the full representation of the Father, not a counterpart. His words are the Father's words. We see what God is like when we look at his Son. These verses are just as true as John 3:16 and Genesis 1.

The Response

The primary response of God showing us his love is that we would love him back. Human beings are the only creature made in his image, the only ones with the right to search out his heart, the only ones filled with his Spirit, and the only creature made to love him. Jesus did not show mercy to the fig tree in Matthew 21:19. It had one opportunity to bear him fruit, it didn't, he cursed it, and it died. He did not give it a chance to repent.

In the law, God chose the spilling of animal's blood to be offered as sacrifices to him. A myriad of angels turned their gaze from him and without a second thought, he cast them from his presence.

16For indeed He does not give aid to angels, but He does give aid to the seed of Abraham (Hebrews 2:16).

However, two human beings sinned, he took on their frame and fought for them all the way to death. And after rising from the dead, he gave the very ones who had killed him access to his heart that they might love him.

The Greatest Commandment

It is no wonder that Jesus said the greatest commandment is to love him and to love those whom he loved. This kind of love was what he embodied and sought to produce in us.

36"Teacher, which *is* the great commandment in the law?"

37Jesus said to him, "'You shall love the LORD your God with all your heart, with all your soul, and with all your mind.' 38This is *the* first and great commandment. 39And *the* second *is* like it: 'You shall love your neighbor as yourself.' 40On these two commandments hang all the Law and the Prophets" (Matthew 22:36-40).

⁹As the Father loved Me, I also have loved you; abide in My love. ¹⁰If you keep My commandments, you will abide in My love, just as I have kept My Father's commandments and abide in His love (John 15:9-10).

When we enter into and encounter the first commandment, to love him and be loved by him, it automatically produces the second commandment in us. And when we live out the second commandment, it will produce the first commandment in others. There is never a point where you are more like Jesus and in agreement with him than when you love others in a way that produces worship. The reason I prophesied over so many people during my time at Starbucks is because I became addicted to seeing people fall in love with him, finding out that he loved them, and feeling his love myself. That little "I love you" in people is what he paid for.

Prophetic Love

One of the greatest prophetic acts you can do is love people in a way that produces worship. When you love a non-Christian and treat them as a brother, you are prophesying to them. We are all enemies of the cross before we pass through the blood of Christ. When you show love to them, you are prophetically saying, "There is coming a day when we will both stand as brothers before the throne and we will love each other with the love of Christ."

A prophetic lifestyle is not giving words of knowledge in a coffee shop or at a cell phone store. It is not praying for the sick. It is not preaching on a street corner. These are all elements and possibilities, but without love, they are nothing.

> [1]Though I speak with the tongues of men and of angels, but have not love, I have become sounding brass or a clanging cymbal. [2]And though I have *the gift of* prophecy, and understand all mysteries and all knowledge, and though I have all faith, so that I could remove mountains, but have not love, I am nothing. [3]And though I bestow all my goods to feed *the poor*, and though I give my body to be burned, but have not love, it profits me nothing (1 Corinthians 13:1-3).

Jesus was, is, and will always be our standard for loving people. When someone hears a statement like that, their first tendency is to think of the cross and what Jesus accomplished there. That is true. Jesus could have come down, died on a cross, rose from the dead, and went back to the throne and that would have been sufficient. Had He done that, though, we wouldn't have seen what it was like for Jesus to love on a daily basis, to be a leader, to respond to accusations, or to be treated as the outcast.

There are so many places in the gospels where we could look at these types of scenarios, but, for the sake of time, we are only going to look at a couple.

> [9]As Jesus passed on from there, He saw a man named Matthew sitting at the tax office. And He said to him, "Follow Me." So he arose and followed Him (Matthew 9:9).

Out of all of the disciples, Matthew was the most unlikely candidate. This was for one reason: he was a tax collector. People in any country aren't usually fans of their government tax officials. In the United States, most people cringe at the sound of the IRS even if they are above reproach in their finances.

In Jerusalem, it was far worse. The Roman Government, the nation that had conquered the Jews, employed the tax collectors. The Jews had a deep and unyielding conviction that God alone was their king. Being a tax collector for another king was considered nothing less than treason.

In fact, by Jewish law, a tax collector was excommunicated from the synagogue and was not allowed to worship at the temple in Jerusalem during the feasts. The Jews even considered them to be unclean, along with all animals and things listed in Leviticus 20:25.

They even considered tax collectors to be in the same class as murderers and robbers. Yet, Jesus saw Matthew in a way that no one else saw him. He did not define Matthew by what he was doing, but by the dreams of his heart. He did not see a man for what he was, but what he could be, and he loved him for it. He loved him in a way that produced worship, honor, and love in return.

¹Then *Jesus* entered and passed through Jericho. ²Now behold, *there was* a man named Zacchaeus who was a chief tax collector, and he was rich. ³And he sought to see who Jesus was, but could not because of the crowd, for he was of short stature. ⁴So he ran ahead and climbed up into a sycamore tree to see Him, for He was going to pass that *way*. ⁵And when Jesus came to the place, He looked up and saw him, and said to him, "Zacchaeus, make haste and come down, for today I must stay at your house." ⁶So he made haste and came down, and received Him joyfully. ⁷But when they saw *it*, they all complained, saying, "He has gone to be a guest with a man who is a sinner."

⁸Then Zacchaeus stood and said to the Lord, "Look, Lord, I give half of my goods to the poor; and if I have taken anything from

anyone by false accusation, I restore fourfold."

9And Jesus said to him, "Today salvation has come to this house, because he also is a son of Abraham; 10for the Son of Man has come to seek and to save that which was lost" (Luke 19:1-10).

Here we see another example of Jesus choosing to love, against all odds. Luke makes sure we know that Zacchaeus was rich, having taken much from the Jews. Not only was he a hated tax collector; he was a rich, hated tax collector. Zacchaeus was trying to press through the crowds to see Jesus. As a tax collector, they would not let him in the synagogue, and there was no way they were going to let him close to Jesus. Being a short guy, he did what he could.

What happens next is outstanding. Jesus calls him by name. No one would acknowledge him, and here Jesus calls his name out above the noise of the crowd, "Zacchaeus!" I can imagine everyone got quiet. Maybe they are thinking that Jesus is about to let him have it, call him out, to tell him to repent or that he is a traitor.

I wonder if Matthew knew what was coming next. Maybe Zacchaeus had heard of Matthew as one of the twelve, and believed Jesus would restore him, as well. All we know is that Jesus calls him by name, and says, "I'm going to your house today to break bread!"

No wonder the people began to grumble. No doubt there were many who considered themselves devout Jews and had been following Jesus for days or more, and Jesus hadn't gone to their house to break bread. We must also understand that in the Middle East, especially during this time, breaking bread with one another was a sign of deep friendship.

This was far more than Jesus going over for burgers and feeling things out. He was calling Zacchaeus friend. Now, notice Zacchaeus' response. Immediately, he begins to do the first and second commandment.

This is prophetic love. This is love that produces worship for God and love for others in return. Then, Jesus takes it one step further. He declares Zacchaeus a son of Abraham. He took a man that was considered as low as a murderer and thief, who was excommunicated from the synagogues and who was dead to the Jews, and called him as a Jew and restored his honor amongst his countrymen.

Jesus loved Zacchaeus for who he could be, not who he had been. He loved him in a way that unlocked the heart of a man who had been locked out from everyone else's. He loved him because he loved him, because he loved him, because he loved him, because he loved him...

Jesus' life defined the prophetic like this: *living life in a way that bears witness of a coming kingdom.* Everything he did, every move he made, every word he spoke provoked in others the opportunity to love the way they would love and be loved for all of eternity. We must take hold of love, because it first took hold of us.

3
WHAT THE HIGH CALLING IS NOT

I started working for Walmart when I was 16 years old. I spent seven years with the company and had various duties, including a long list of supervisory positions. I had everything going for me at a young age. I specifically remember visiting at an executive's house one night. He said, "Michael, you write whatever amount of money you want to earn on this check right here, and you'll make it, and I'll help you do it with this company."

We had grand plans for my future with the company, but I had a major dilemma going on inside of me. I felt called to ministry. I loved teaching, preaching and leading worship. But, I only knew two types of men: businessmen and ministers. I had no grid for a man that was successful in business and had a furious love for God. I did not know that both could exist, so I quit my job and went full time into ministry.

Most are under the assumption that full time ministry is the highest form of Christianity. Most of us grew up, and many still live this way, believing that our pastors, worship leaders, and missionaries were the elite of the faith. We looked at the way they preached and sang, heard the stories of their missions, and automatically assumed that in order to get where they were, we had to do what they had done. I see this happen all the time.

Young men and women see a man or woman of God that they admire functioning in full time ministry. Then, they believe that the only way to get to that point of authority and faith is to abandon everything and go into "the ministry." We read the stories of the disciples, and we see that James and John left fishing. Matthew left the taxing business. All of the other disciples left what they were doing and followed Jesus. We assume that we are to do the same.

At that time, the culture in Israel warranted such a thing worthy to do. Becoming a Rabbi (which is what they initially thought they were leaving their vocations for) was considered the highest calling, aside from being born into the priesthood. Their fathers would have gladly let them go to follow Christ and picked up the slack in the family business.

Today, we live in a different time and place. The majority of our nation does not go to church during the week. However, the majority of the nation works, shops, goes to movies, eats out, drinks coffee, buys cars, goes to the doctor's office, and so on. The point is that most people feel as though they are second rate Christians in comparison to full time "ministers." They assume that working a job 40 or 50 hours a week is their meaningless lot in life, perhaps only good for funding the "real" Christians found pastoring Churches, leading worship, or reaching out as missionaries to the nations.

Many feel as though their worth to the body of Christ depends upon the size of their checkbook. Not only is that insulting, but it is not biblical. When we remember the widow's mite, we see that she gave less than everyone in the natural, but more than most in the spiritual. The truth is, you can get far more ministry done during a 40 to 50 hour workweek than you can during an hour at church. The best part about it is that you don't have to invite them to come! They are already getting paid to be there!

The "high calling" is not to serve full time in a church, give all your money away, live poor, save souls daily, intercede long hours, preach, teach, lead worship, serve the poor, heal the sick, adopt orphans, or whatever else that comes to your mind. All of these things are callings of the Lord, but not one of them is "the high calling."

What Is The High Calling?

The good news is that there is no such thing as the "highest calling" of God in scripture. Not once do we see God look at a man in scripture and say, "Look at this man everyone. Look at what he is doing. This is the high calling and everything else is secondary." He did not say it of Moses the deliverer, David the king, Isaiah the prophet, Paul the apostle, or even John the beloved. Never once does it list that there is one vocation that all Christians should be doing.

That would supersede the reality of the Body of Christ. There is a reason that Jesus is the head of the body and we make up the rest of its members. If Jesus, the head, only had a body made of hands it would be highly ineffective. To assume that one part of the body was somehow more important than the rest would be like telling the arm it should have been a foot, and that every member of the body should follow suit. It wouldn't work.

Unfortunately, many of us have believed that, because we were not a hand or a foot, that somehow we are less important and hold less value in the body of Christ. Have you ever jammed a finger, stubbed a pinky toe or gotten a paper cut? Did you lose any ability in that member of your body? Do you remember how it affected you and caused you to be less efficient at certain tasks? Do you remember how inconvenient that one little injury was?

The human body is comprised of numerous members, all with unique functions that work together, controlled by one mind and sustained by one heart. As long as each one is connected to the heart and obedient to the mind, it will function properly. We, as the body of Christ, are no different. If each individual member is not connected to the Head, which is Christ, and sustained by the love of God and who he is, we will be weaker and less effective in our arena of the kingdom. We have to ask a different question…

What Is My Highest Calling?

Your highest calling is different than everyone else's. Moses had a different calling than David. Moses was not called to replace Saul. David was not called to lead Israel into a different land. Isaiah's message was different than Ezekiel's message. Not one of these men of God had the high calling of God… They had their calling.

The highest calling of God is being obedient to whatever the Lord calls you to do, wherever he places you to do it, for however long he calls you to do it. To be obedient to the Lord's call is love.

Has God called you to be a CEO? Great! Has God called you to wash toilets? Great! Do it and love him while you're at it. Are you a Mom? Great! Then love your kids as though they are Christ. There are innumerable high callings in the body of Christ.

He has redeemed us by the blood of the Lamb and made us to be priests and kings in his kingdom. He does not separate kings and priests by earthly incomes, but by eternal currency. What is our eternal currency? It is obedient love. If you are responsible with earthly things he will give you heavenly things. It is not merely obedience in the realm of tasks, ministry, or works.

If you do them without love, they don't count. In the letter to Ephesus, the Lord said, "You are doing great works. They are awesome! But you have forgotten the most important thing. You have forgotten your first love." This is why we are kings and priests, not just kings and not just priests. If we were only kings we would only be doing tasks and running a kingdom.

We would become detached from Christ, and we would begin to think our kingdom was our own. We would revel in our own glory. On the other hand, if we were only priests, we would never get any kingdom work done. We would continually be in the temple, neglecting the economy of the kingdom, its business, and normal everyday requirements. As both kings and priests, we minister to him, worship him, love him, encounter him and help establish his kingdom on the earth.

We are all kings and priests before him. I've met men and women who operate primarily in the king mode and know nothing of the priest mode. They get a lot of work done, but miss the excitement of doing it with him and encountering his heart. They grow bitter, self-reliant, and, in many cases, end up lacking the heart of Christ in regards to their finances. I've also met many who function primarily in the priest mode. They end up missing most of life's normal everyday tasks. They love God, but everything around them is in disarray.

You don't have to be a CEO or a pastor to be a king or a priest. Your job does not designate your calling. Your calling operates in and around what you do. Scripture does not say we are a kingdom of kings or priests, but of kings and priests. If a CEO does not operate as a priest before the Lord, he will lose the heart of God for his business and his employees.

If a pastor does not operate as a king before the Lord, he will lose his authority and become dependent upon everyone else, make poor decisions, and run a disorganized ministry. There are janitors that are manifesting their highest calling in God as kings and priests. There are moms who are operating in their highest calling in God as kings and priests. The janitor must see his building as his kingdom that he stewards, the place that he meets with God.

The guy making coffee must see his coffee shop as the place that he brings the kingdom of God. The place where he has authority and the altar that he ministers to the Lord upon. This is more than a poetic thought or paradigm. This is reality in Christ's kingdom. Everything counts if it is done in obedient love.

How Do I Know What My High Calling Is?

This is a question that no book, pastor, friend, parent, or mentor can answer for you. There is no blanket answer for your life. In fact, your life will consist of numerous callings and season changes. Each calling will remain as you move on to the next phase of life. Your calling is not who you are, it is simply something the Lord wants to do with you.

Many base their identity off of what they do vocationally or someone else's accomplishment or anointing. The result is a lifelong identity crisis that creates insecurity and a lack of courage to move on to the next thing in life. In this, there is only a constant sense of failure. You are a king and a priest no matter what you are doing, if you are doing it in obedient love. Your calling never changes; the way it looks will. Let me explain:

In the winter you wear a coat, in the spring you'll wear a light jacket (depending on where you live), in the summer you'll wear shorts, and in the fall you may wear a sweater. Different seasons of life will require different acts of obedient love. I had a season in life where I was called to be in a prayer room 30 hours a week. The time came when that season changed and I did not want to change with it. I did not want to move on into the next season God had for me.

During that season, I hit a plateau in my growth in the Lord. No matter what I did, it seemed as though I wasn't progressing. I still loved God and he loved me, but it was like I hit a wall. One day, I was asking the Lord what the problem was, and he said to me, "It's summer, and you still have your winter coat on."

I realized that I had become comfortable in my last season, but the Lord had called me into something else. When I responded to the Lord and began to move on, I saw an increase in anointing, in my teaching, worship leading, and my prophetic ministry.

This season, God may have called you to work extra hours to store up money, pay off debt, or fund a missionary. He may have called you to switch jobs. He may have called you to stay at a job you don't care for because of your boss or coworkers. You are probably asking, "How do I know, or how do I find out, what God as called me to do?" Only you will know, and you will find out by doing the first and second commandment.

That probably seems too simple to most. But the scripture says that he directs all your paths and makes them straight. Even when you make a wrong turn, the kindness of God will move you back on track, as though you never went off.

As a father, I love to watch my children play. Their play is their work. They are so serious building with blocks, putting their dolls to bed, feeding them, "shopping" at their store, and cooking dinner in their oven.

I love watching! I let them continue doing whatever it is they are doing until they are about to do something that could potentially harm them. I help them to avoid it. I help them understand the consequences, so that they know why I intervened, and that I have their best interests and safety in mind. If I am this way with my kids and I'm a new dad and a fallen man, then how much more will the Father do for us?

What Will Happen When You Embrace This?

You will begin to see the kingdom of God advance through what you do. When you enter into the place of obedient love, you create a connecting point between heaven and earth. You give the Holy Spirit an outlet to move through you wherever you are doing whatever it is you are doing (we will look at this more in another chapter). The atmosphere at work around you will change as your heart is engaged in worship. You will have an eternal impact on the people around you because you will be bringing his presence into the workplace.

Most Christians' discontentment at work is due to the fact that it feels like a waste of time. We have to shift the way we view our workplace and the way we view ourselves. The truth is, you go on a ministry trip every day. The truth is, you are a king and priest, and your throne is the chair you sit in at your cubby. Your altar is the desk you work at, your scepter is your mop, and your royal goblet is your cup of coffee.

When you begin making this paradigm shift, the way you view your workplace changes. Your workplace will become the place you have dominion over. It will become the place you go to meet with God, to encounter his heart, to see people fall in love with him, and to see his kingdom established.

4

CONSTANT COMMUNION

Breathe

We take in about 21,600 breaths a day. That is about 88 pounds of oxygen. We are naturally supposed to breathe from our abdominal, but due to stress, exercise, anxiety, tiredness, etc., we typically breathe from our chest, which makes us take in less oxygen. This is what causes us to sigh or yawn. We actually remove 70% of our toxins and derive 90% of our energy by breathing.

It is a central part of what we do, even when we are unaware that it is taking place. Probably even as you are reading this you are becoming aware of your breathing, its patterns, its depth, frequency, and the air's movement in and out of you.

In Exodus, Moses goes up the mountain to see a bush that is burning without being consumed. We know the story well. When he arrives at the location, the Lord tells him to take off his shoes because he is on holy ground.

It wasn't that when Moses got there, the ground suddenly became holy; it was that Moses was made aware of it. After Moses accepted the Lord's commission to deliver Israel, fear overcame Moses, and he said, "Indeed, when I come to the children of Israel and say to them, 'The God of your fathers has sent me to you,' and they say to me, 'What is his name?' what shall I say to them?" And God said to Moses, "I AM WHO I AM."

In some translations of the Bible, the Lord's response is translated L O R D. The actual translation is four Hebraic consonants *Y H V H*. They are pronounced *Yo-Hey-Vah-Hey*. In many Hebrew cultures, they will not write this on paper, post it on the Internet, or speak it because it is so holy. In some ancient rabbinical teachings, they said the consonants are pronounced so lightly that the Lord's response simply sounded like breathing.

In other words, Moses said, "What is your name?" and God simply breathed. Is the name of God breath? In Genesis, it says that God breathed life into Adam. The Hebrew word for breath is "*ruach*." In the New Testament the same word is translated "*pneuma*" for Spirit. Paul went so far as to say that the Spirit, the "*pneuma*" or "*ruach*," lives inside of us.

[16]Do you not know that you are the temple of God and *that* the Spirit of God dwells in you (1 Corinthians 3:16)?

[19]Or do you not know that your body is the temple of the Holy Spirit *who* is in you, whom you have from God, ... (1 Corinthians 6:19A)

The Holy breath, or, Holy Spirit, is alive and moving in us. The "*ruach*" is the "*pneuma*" who lives inside of us and is moving with every breath. This being true, we must ask ourselves this question... Are we standing on Holy Ground all the time?

We typically think that the first thing a baby has to do when it is born is breathe or cry. Does it have to breathe on its own, or does it have to say the name of God?

When a man dies, is it because he can no longer breathe? Or does he cease to live when he can no longer say the name of God? Is the spirit of God moving in and through you all the time? Are you just becoming aware of it right now?

Have you had to listen to a friend, family member, or co-worker say, "There... is... no... God"? Maybe if you listen closely you might actually hear them say, "Yo... Hey... Vah... Hey."

It is in him that we live and move and have our being every moment of every day. We pass burning bushes all the time. You work next to them, manage them, parent them, buy your food from them, and speak with them. They just don't know who they are, and most of the time, we forget who we are and who is in us.

The Personal Effect

Even as I am writing this, I remember to "breathe." Instantly I feel him. There is a slight smile that is crossing my face as I feel his nearness to me. How kind of God! So much about staying in the place of constant communion is being aware of his presence. In a single breath you can be in his presence.

He is not far off, and he is not waiting for you to come to him by fighting through a list of repentance, pressing through the heavens, battling demons, and moving past the angels. He is closer than your skin. When realizing his nearness, it causes us to respond and not react, to have courage and not back down, to have faith and not fear, to love and not lament.

The same Spirit that lives inside of you hovered over the waters at creation, appeared in a cloud of smoke and fire, fell upon Mt. Carmel, consumed Solomon's Altar, rested on the prophets, descended upon Christ, and raised him from the dead. Something incredible happens when we encounter the truth that lives inside of us, at work, at home, and throughout our day. Suddenly, the things we had considered to be mountains, look more like molehills.

Our confidence grows, and our desire to talk about, and encounter him burns in us a fresh.

The Corporate Effect

When you begin to stay in the place of constant communion, it has a spiritual and a tangible effect on your workplace. It is impossible to affect the spiritual atmosphere of your workplace and not see its effect on the people and the business. The spiritual and the natural are not separate forces at work. They directly affect each other.

When the spiritual atmosphere of a place changes, the natural things (people, attitudes, business) in that place are affected either positively or negatively. When the presence of God came to Solomon's Temple look what happened.

> ¹When Solomon had finished praying, fire came down from heaven and consumed the burnt offering and the sacrifices; and the glory of the LORD filled the temple. ²And the priests could not enter the house of the LORD, because the glory of the LORD had filled the LORD's house (2 Chronicles 7:1-2).

One translation says that the priests could not stand up and were laying down all around the temple. I'm not saying that, as you commune with the Lord, the presence is going to come so strong that everyone in your office is going to fall on the floor, incapacitated, and not be able to work. However, as you continue to engage with the Lord at work or at home, it is inevitable that change will begin to take place, and the people there will be affected.

Why? Because you create a meeting place with God and it is impossible for God to show up and not affect an atmosphere and the people around. The most common results we see throughout the Word is that people began to worship, change occurred, and people began to call on the name of the Lord. Abraham was a pagan. He did not know God and most likely worshiped idols. But the Lord came and encountered Abraham with his presence.

What was Abraham's response? He built an altar (this was a lot of work) and worshiped. Moses committed murder and fled Egypt. Yet when the Lord encountered him, he had courage to go back to Egypt.

Saul in his wickedness could not help but prophesy when he came into the presence. Israel would repent time and time again. When people encountered the love of Christ, they worshipped him. And Jesus promised that when the Holy Spirit came he would do this very thing amongst the people.

> [8]And when He has come, He will convict the world of sin, and of righteousness, and of judgment: [9]of sin, because they do not believe in Me; [10]of righteousness, because I go to My Father and you see Me no more; [11]of

judgment, because the ruler of this world is judged (John 16:8-11).

When I started working at Starbucks, the atmosphere was filled with complaining, arguing, and grumbling. I chose to abstain from entering those conversations. When asked what I thought, I gave short "blah" answers. Over time, the conversations started to change. Theology and other in-depth conversations became the norm, and the Holy Spirit always gave wisdom, peace, and utterance during those talks. One time, a new girl (who desperately needed Jesus) was watching me prophesy over someone and asked another barista what I was doing.

They told her, and she laughed as though it was a joke and went back to work. A few days later, she happened to be on break while I was prophesying over a young man. The presence of the Lord was very strong. I didn't know she was listening to the whole thing, including the young man's response and emotions. When she got off of break, she went back to the same barista and said in the most serious voice and with a shell-shocked look, "He talks to God!"

Her attitude at work began to change, and her conversations began to be more and more deep and inquisitive. Later, she even asked me if I could prophesy over her. She wanted an encounter with God.

We had a guy named Rob who came in every morning and bought a "venti, soy, chai." I noticed, as time went on, that he would come in sometimes during the day and just sit.

Some mornings he would come in, sit, and close his eyes. He told me later that he didn't know what it was, but there was something about coming into our Starbucks that made him be at peace. He said it didn't matter how bad of a day or week he was having. He could come to our store, sit down, and be at peace.

When I first started working at AT&T, the conversation was vulgar, filled with profanity, and lacked depth of any sort. I asked the Lord for another Christian to work with. Two weeks later, a guy named Jeremiah Isaiah got hired, and he also loved the Lord. We began to ask the Lord to come to our work and manifest his presence. We would encourage each other via email, and talked openly about the Lord with each other during work.

Within the year, a woman who was involved in various ungodly things began going to church and listening to nothing but worship music. A guy who had a child with his girlfriend he was living with began to discuss his convictions with us, started going to church, and got married. Another girl who worked there actually asked to be prophesied over. A young man began to tell me that he needed the Lord.

My manager began to ask me if I had any recent stories, because he liked hearing them. The language began to cease, and the conversations found their way more and more towards the Lord.

Most people that have full time jobs spend more time with the people they work with than they spend with their family, church friends, or even at church.

If we don't enter into the place of constant communion at work, that means we will spend the majority of our week without feeling the Lord, speaking to him, encountering him, and allowing those around us the most to be affected by his presence. The best part about this: He wants to encounter them with his presence!

How Do I Do This?

The first thing to do is to ask the Lord to increase your desire for him. You may feel provoked right now to begin moving into this. You may be in a place where your heart is unmoved by much and your spirit is dry from the last season. So ask.

24Until now you have asked nothing in My name. Ask, and you will receive, that your joy may be full (John 16:24).

2... you do not have because you do not ask (James 4:2B).

However, we can't completely spiritualize this. Remember, the spiritual and the natural are not separate. The Lord calls us to love him with all of our mind, as well as our spirit. We need practical ways to remind us to engage with the Lord, especially if this is something that we have not practiced. He will give us grace, but we have to do our part as well.

> [37]Jesus said to him, "You shall love the LORD your God with all your heart, with all your soul, and with all your mind." (Matthew 22:37).

Leave yourself reminders: sticky notes, Microsoft Outlook reminders, reminders on your cell phone, turn worship on at work if you have that option, give yourself a Bible verse to recite and memorize each day, just say, "I love you Jesus" when you get a chance, pray in the spirit, or just breathe. If you have someone at work that is a Christian, get together to pray once or twice a week before work. Ask the Lord to bring his presence to your workplace or home. He wants to come and encounter you, and he will not ignore your request to meet with him.

> [7]Ask, and it will be given to you; seek, and you will find; knock, and it will be opened to you. [8]For everyone who asks receives, and he who seeks finds, and to him who knocks it will be opened. [9]Or what man is there among you who, if his son asks for bread, will give him a stone? [10]Or if he asks for a fish, will he give him a serpent? [11]If you then, being evil,

know how to give good gifts to your children, how much more will your Father who is in heaven give good things to those who ask Him (Matthew 7:7-11)!

Entering into the place of constant communion takes time and will come in waves. There are still days that I get through and realize, I was so busy with work, that I had almost no mindful interaction with him. We cannot let those days get us down, or make us feel like we failed. It matters that you want to be meeting with him and spending your day with him.

He is fully aware of the movements of your heart, even the weak ones. He knows that your spirit is willing and your body is weak. This doesn't surprise him. Your simple "I love you" during the midst of a workday, or after a workday, was worth everything to him. It is what he paid for. He had the angels. He wanted you.

5

REDEFINING A PROPHETIC LIFESTYLE

When most people think of a prophetic lifestyle, they think of the power gifts, healing, evangelism, prophecy, third heaven encounters, and Acts 2 type events of epic proportions. We read the great stories of John G. Lake, Smith Wigglesworth, George Whitfield, and think anything less is not a true prophetic lifestyle. Again, we must shift our perspective.

Most of the biographies written about these men focus on the events that took place in their lives and not the everyday lifestyle they cultivated in order to maintain the level of anointing and power they walked in. We have to remember that the stories in the book of Acts took place over years, and the stories of the heroes of the faith we read about took place over a lifetime. The fruit of your lifestyle validates the gifts you operate in. Your gifts will be remembered, but your fruit will remain.

Let us define a prophetic lifestyle this way: *living life in a way that bears witness of a coming kingdom.*

Dwelling On Earth as Citizens of Heaven

"Christians are indistinguishable from other men either by nationality, language or customs. They do not inhabit separate cities of their own, or speak a strange dialect, or follow some outlandish way of life. Their teaching is not based upon reveries inspired by the curiosity of men. Unlike some other people, they champion no purely human doctrine. With regard to dress, food and manner of life in general, they follow the customs of whatever city they happen to be living in, whether it is Greek or foreign.

"And yet there is something extraordinary about their lives. They live in their own countries as though they were only passing through. They play their full role as citizens, but labor under all the disabilities of aliens. Any country can be their homeland, but for them their homeland, wherever it may be, is a foreign country. Like others, they marry and have children, but they do not expose them. They share their meals, but not their wives.

"They live in the flesh, but they are not governed by the desires of the flesh. They pass their days upon earth, but they are citizens of heaven. …"

—From a letter to Diognetus

This quote was written between the end of the 2nd century and beginning of the 3rd century. It is debated over who Diognetus was. It is possible that he was a tutor of Marcus Aurelius, the Roman emperor, or a procurator for Alexandria. This was taken from a letter that had been written to him by another official, questioning why they were persecuting Christians. His observations are astounding. He almost quotes the apostle Paul.

[20]For our citizenship is in heaven, from which we also eagerly wait for the Savior, the Lord Jesus Christ (Philippians 3:20),

The people that he had seen in various countries that called on the name of Christ lived in such a manner that he actually called them citizens of heaven. Notice that he did not say they were preaching on every street corner, healing the sick, raising the dead, or evangelizing a city. He spoke of their lifestyle. There is a way of life that we can live, are called to live, and will live out forever, that is in this world and not of it. It can and will affect every arena of life if we will embrace it.

An Extreme Paradigm?

We have to ask, "What do citizens of heaven look like?" A further look into Diognetus' observation would tell us what he saw. However, we do not stand before the judgment seat of Diognetus when we die, nor did he die on a cross for our sins. We have one standard we live by, and that is Christ's.

Even before looking at citizens of heaven, we must understand that there are two kingdoms on the earth, and really only two types of citizens on earth, as well.

There is the Kingdom of God, ruled by Christ, and there is the kingdom of this world, ruled and influenced by Satan.

> [19]We know that we are of God, and the whole world lies *under the sway of* the wicked one (1 John 5:19).

> [13]He has delivered us from the power of darkness and conveyed *us* into the kingdom of the Son of His love (Colossians 1:13),

The way that we live represents and agrees with one of these kingdoms rules and principles. This does not mean that because you sin you are a citizen of Satan's kingdom. I am talking about areas of your heart in which you are not pursuing the Lord and are allowing the enemy to wreak havoc in your life. If you believe the name of Jesus, that he is God's perfect son, who died on the cross for your sins, rose from the dead, sent the Holy Spirit and you are walking this out, then you are a citizen of heaven.

However, that is just the entry point to the kingdom of God. We want to move into the fullness of what he has for us. The enemy is committed to keeping us from this, especially in the marketplace.

Many people went to a Christian camp growing up, or have been to a weekend retreat. If you have ever worked at a church full time, you'll know this as well. It is easier to live like a Christian when you're around other Christians. It's easier not to complain, murmur, slander, speak profanely or impure, when you around people who do not complain, murmur, slander, speak profanely and impurely. These are not supposed to be a part of a Christian lifestyle.

Most Christians know that and provoke each other to righteousness. In the market place, it is usually the opposite. People use profanity, speak perversely, lie, backstab, complain, murmur, slander, and take part in various ungodly activities outside of work. They live this way because they are operating under the leadership and laws of a kingdom that you are not a part of. They are not citizens of heaven (yet). They are under the leadership and influence of a king that you do not serve.

You might feel convicted right now. You may be thinking that you have already failed at this and blown your witness at work. Have I failed at this before? Absolutely! You must remember that you are not defined by your failures. You are defined by how he loves you. Remember that when Peter defined himself by his actions he lived in shame; but when he allowed Jesus to define him by love, he shook Jerusalem.

I've seen many Christians become upset with the people they work with because of their lifestyle, and they react by telling them they are going to go to hell or will be judged. This is neither Christ-like nor biblical. Paul did not preach to the Gentiles that they were sinning and needed to stop. He preached Christ, the Holy Spirit brought conviction, and people were saved, then he continued to disciple churches.

Jesus did not come to the Gentiles, or even Israel, preaching their sin to them. In fact, the only time Jesus preached any sort of judgment, it was in regards to the religious leaders of the day who were leading the people astray. The prophets of the Old Testament did not go to the nations outside of Israel who were worshipping idols and tell them they were wrong and were going to Hades.

Paul's letters were to believers, Jesus' teachings were to worshippers of YWHW (the God of Israel), and the prophet's judgments and calls to righteousness were to Israel as well. Israel was to be a light, a sign, and a wonder to the world, and cause the world to turn their eyes to God. We see this happen in the Exodus. There were Egyptians who saw how the Lord acted on behalf of Israel and many left Egypt with them. Egyptians left to worship the God of Israel in the desert because of God's protection and favor over Israel during the plagues.

> [37]Then the children of Israel journeyed from Rameses to Succoth, about six hundred thousand men on foot, besides children. [38]A mixed multitude went up with them also, … (Exodus 12:37-38A)

When Paul wrote to the Gentiles in Romans, he said that the call of the Christian gentiles was to provoke unbelieving Jews to jealousy that they would come to Christ and be saved. Christ came to draw all men unto him, not convict all men unto himself.

> [13]For I speak to you Gentiles; inasmuch as I am an apostle to the Gentiles, I magnify my ministry, [14]if by any means I may provoke to jealousy *those who are* my flesh and save some of them (Romans 11:13-14).

> [32]And I, if I am lifted up from the earth, will draw all *peoples* to Myself" (John 12:32).

When I was in Seoul, Korea, I was bewildered by the driving in their city. Pedestrians don't stop for cars, and cars don't really stop for pedestrians. It's amazing that the people driving scooters are alive for more than a few blocks. People drive up roads the wrong way and sometimes turn where they need to, regardless of what the signs say. In America, there would have been tickets written all over the place.

People would have been upset, honking horns, making other gestures, and comments out of their car windows. But, they weren't in America. They were in Korea. They weren't under American authority or in American culture. They were under South Korean authority and culture, so I didn't expect them to live like they were under American rule. We, as citizens of heaven, cannot expect citizens of another kingdom to live like they are citizens of heaven.

We are to live out our citizenship under the authority, culture, and favor of our king in such a way that it provokes those around us to jealousy. This includes things like: not complaining, not gossiping or slandering, submitting to your authorities at work, having a good work ethic, serving and helping those you work with, abstaining from ungodly activities and conversations in and out of work, and walking in joy.

Submitting to the authority at your work, as though they were the Lord, is one of the greatest witnesses you can exemplify, as well as one of the fastest ways to gain authority in the place of prayer over your workplace. No matter where I have worked, it has been normal to complain and slander the manager. I have had my fair share of supervisors and I can't say that I didn't agree with them. But the Lord calls us to a much higher standard.

I must go on a bunny trail here for a moment to mention my manager, who gave me the freedom to do what I did at Starbucks. His name was Jeff Page. This was a man who ran his Starbucks as Jesus would have. He would go on extended fasts during his 60-hour work weeks at Starbucks. His management, integrity, and love for Christ, I believe, is what provided the spiritual atmosphere for me to do what I did. I recall one time a well-known leader of a ministry came through.

The girl running the register asked Jeff if he was going to get his drink for him. The girl was thinking that Jeff was going to just give him the drink free of charge. Instead, Jeff pulled out his wallet and paid for the minister's drink.

I have worked for many managers, but I have never seen anyone exemplify Christ as a manager in the way Jeff Page did. I am grateful for the opportunity he gave me during our time together.

17And whatever you do in word or deed, *do* all in the name of the Lord Jesus, giving thanks to God the Father through Him. ... 23And whatever you do, do it heartily, as to the Lord and not to men (Colossians 3:17 & 23),

In whatever we do, we do it unto the Lord. It doesn't say, "When serving the poor, or preaching a sermon, or leading worship, or witnessing." It says "in whatever we do, do it as to the Lord." This includes submitting to our ungodly managers.

When 1 Peter was written, the government of Rome was already persecuting the church. Not once does Peter call the church to boycott the government, protest, or cry out against it. Instead, he gives them the most peculiar instruction.

> [13]Therefore submit yourselves to every ordinance of man for the Lord's sake, whether to the king as supreme, [14]or to governors, … [15]For this is the will of God, that by doing good you may put to silence the ignorance of foolish men— [16]as free, yet not using liberty as a cloak for vice, but as bondservants of God. [17]Honor all *people*. Love the brotherhood. Fear God. Honor the king.
>
> [18]Servants, *be* submissive to *your* masters with all fear, not only to the good and gentle, but also to the harsh (1 Peter 2:13-14A & 15-18).

Peter's instruction is simple. Submit to all leadership. Honor those over you and those around you. It is no doubt that many of the Christians in Rome read this and were perplexed. Christians were dying, pagans were running the city, perversity and immorality ran freely, and the people lived without conviction. They were probably hoping for a letter of action.

However, Peter told them to honor all people and honor the king, Nero. This is the same emperor who would use Christians as human torches to light his gardens at night. Remember, this is the same disciple that drew a sword and tried to take a man's head off! Jesus walked this out to the fullest measure.

He walked this out all the way to the cross. It was his submissions that led him to the cross and ultimately put him in the position, as a man, to conquer death. It was Jesus' full submission to the governmental authorities, without sin in his heart, which gave him authority over all governments. Peter understood a primary law of the kingdom: *When we live as Christ, it invites his presence.*

The only thing that Peter ever asked Jesus to teach him was how to pray (at least that is recorded in scripture). In Jesus' blueprint prayer, he said, "… let it be on earth as it is in heaven." The entirety of the Lord's Prayer was focused on a one on one relationship with the Father. So, to think that this one line in the prayer applies directly to anything else is out of context.

Jesus said to pray, "Let it be with me, on earth as it is in heaven. Let me live, talk, work, love, eat, pray, worship, and have a lifestyle on earth as it is in heaven (my interpretation). Give me grace to walk as though I am forever before you in your city and manifest your kingdom around me." Jesus submitted to all leadership.

His entire life, he went to the synagogue every Sabbath and sat under the teaching of the law that he wrote. He was taught how to work the carpentry tools that he created. He submitted to the law perfectly (613 commandments). He submitted to the mother and father that he picked, designed and created. He did all things unto the Father in love.

Imagine the humility in the submission of Jesus. He had a mental history and recollection of his eternal history with the Father and still submitted to leadership, authorities, and even death on a cross.

> [5]And now, O Father, glorify Me together with Yourself, with the glory which I had with You before the world was (John 17:5).

He is our standard. He is our goal. He is our way. Our goal is not to prophesy over people daily, pray for the sick, or evangelize. Our goal is to exemplify Christ, engage his heart, and bring heaven to earth. Christ walked in a perpetual state of obedience to the Father, sensitivity and communion with the Holy Spirit, and love.

Every day he lived, he bought us access to his presence in every arena of life. When the bill was full and complete, he paid for it on the cross. We will look at this more in the next chapter. It is crucial to understand the he has already done this and made a way for us to walk it out.

6
SAYING YES TO NAZARETH

He could have picked anywhere in the world to grow up, and he chose Nazareth. He could have chosen Jerusalem or Rome, gathered crowds at a young age, and been known as the Messiah his entire life. But he chose Nazareth, a small, isolated town of a few families. Nathaniel asked, "Can anything good come out of Nazareth?" Jesus Christ would forever answer that question.

Why would he choose a place that was as poor and forgotten as this town? He would receive no recognition for his accomplishments. He would not be noticed at all, yet day after day he would say yes to living in Nazareth; day after day he would say yes to the Father. It was the thirty years of saying yes in Nazareth that prepared him to say yes in Gethsemane.

Many people want to say yes to the Lord in the place of martyrdom, but do not want to say yes to the Lord in the everyday things of life. They aren't willing to say yes to living where the Lord has called them to live, or say yes to working the job they are called to work. Yet, they expect themselves to say yes in the bigger things.

Once in college, when I was still with Walmart, I was throwing boxes in a warehouse. I was praying and feeling the presence of the Lord. My faith was up and I felt as though I would do anything for the Lord. I was even saying out loud, "Lord, tell me where to go and I'll go. I'll go to Africa. I'll go overseas. I'll go into mission work."

And as I was praying, the Lord interrupted me and said, "Would you work in this warehouse for the next eight years if I asked you to?" I was devastated. My faith dropped. I realized that I would not. He did not ask me to, but he wanted to reveal my heart in the matter. Then he said, "My son said yes to this."

Jesus said yes to being hidden, submitting to the law he wrote, and to the Pharisees he would later rebuke, working as a carpenter in a small town that needed little business, and obeying the parents that he had chosen. It was saying yes 10,000 times when no one was watching that prepared his heart to say yes when the salvation of humanity was hanging in the balance. If you'll say yes to Nazareth, you'll say yes in Gethsemane.

For some, they feel like they go to work in Nazareth every day. They feel like no one notices the floors they mop, the drinks they make, the good job they do taking calls in their cubby, or the hard work they do as a stay at home mom. Those moments, days, and months that feel like that are exactly why Jesus chose Nazareth. He walked in a perpetual state of obedience to the Father, sensitivity, and communion with the Holy Spirit, and love in every arena of life and the heart.

He did it every day and he did it as a man. He wanted to give us access to his presence while taking out the trash, getting a drink of water, taking care of our family, working for an unappreciative client, or having a plain old tough day. With every step he took, with every person he responded to with love, and with every job he did, he gave us the victory and access to his heart in those moments.

We must take off our "God" lenses in order to let the weight and the joy of this hit our spirits. Let me explain. It is easy for us to think of Jesus as God. We don't understand it. But for some reason, it is easier for the words "Jesus is God" to come off our lips than "Jesus is a man." It helps us understand and justifies the fact that he performed countless miracles, walked on water, raised the dead, died on a cross, rose from the dead, and was transfigured on a mountain top.

We expect God to be able to do those things with ease. Why wouldn't we? He's God, right? But God coming in the flesh was not meant to be understood or justified. It was meant to create worship and provoke us to love him. The difficulty in understanding and grabbing a hold of the life of Christ for the average believer is not that Christ is God. That revelation comes from the Holy Spirit and is part of our confession.

The difficulty is believing that Jesus is also fully man, just like us. He invaded our humanity with full force and did not spare any part of it from the divine experience.

> 6who, being in the form of God, did not consider it robbery to be equal with God, 7but made Himself of no reputation, taking the form of a bondservant, *and* coming in the likeness of men. 8And being found in appearance as a man, He humbled Himself and became obedient to *the point of* death, even the death of the cross (Philippians 2:6-8).

It is easy to think that God (Jesus) was in constant communion with the Father and the Holy Spirit, but it strips us of the victory that Jesus fought for on a daily basis. We always pray things like, "God, give me grace to love my co-workers," or "God, give me grace to be patient." The reason that grace is accessible and available to you is because

Jesus, as a man, loved his co-workers with no sin in him. He was patient, even unto death.

Every time Jesus loved someone who wronged him, worked as unto the Lord, served his family and sinned not, he did as a man. It was as a man, he conquered every arena of the heart on a daily basis, so he could meet with you in those places, and give you victory in them so you could experience his presence just like he experienced his Father's.

Living under Accusation

Anytime you are living under the favor of the Lord, there is a measure of accusation that will rise up around you. The enemy will try to discredit you amongst your peers, Christians, and the world. He will take the weak things in your life and magnify them to those around you in the workplace by putting you in situations where those things are most likely to surface. Many have this grand idea of God's favor being all champagne and ticker tape parades.

However, some of the most "favored" men and women in the Bible experienced anything but that for prolonged periods of time. Noah lived in constant persecution and mocking for 120 years. Joseph was sold as a slave by his own family, then thrown in prison unjustly, long before stepping into his destiny. Job was ridden with boils, lost his sons and daughters, and almost all of his possessions overnight because he was the "favored of the Lord" among the earth.

Many of the prophets were beaten, beheaded, sawn in two, stoned to death, or died in other various ways. Then, there is Mary, the highly favored one, mother of Jesus. This is where we will stay for a short while. The film that came out a few years ago, "The Nativity," was the first film I had seen that gave a small glimpse into the cultural dilemma that Mary would have experienced.

In our day, it is normal to have a teen get pregnant out of wedlock. The overhanging shame, in many ways, has been left behind, depending on the girl and the town she lives in. People view the situation as a mistake that they will have to live with and that is about the full extent of it. In Mary's day this was a different story. In the film, Joseph has a dream in which he sees Mary about to be stoned to death.

This is not far off. Not only was she pregnant, but also her only defense was that God, who found her highly favored, did it supernaturally. In a town of 28 to 40 families, that would live their whole lives in Nazareth, this story would not be forgotten. Joseph is never mentioned in the Gospels past the birth of Christ. Many theologians believe that Joseph probably died during Jesus' teen years.

In our day, we view this as a tragedy. In Jesus' day, they probably viewed this as judgmental. This would have only added fuel to the fire of controversy surrounding his birth. Day after day, during his life in Nazareth, he would be under the stigma that he was conceived out of wedlock, and his parents concocted an outrageous story to save their hides.

He would be subject to gossip, slander, and accusation, his entire upbringing. If Joseph did die during Jesus' teen years, imagine the accusation around his death.

"His father was dying and Jesus' couldn't do anything to save him? And he is supposed to be from God?" Imagine the doubt within his family. It says later in the gospels that even his own brothers did not believe him. Was this perhaps what put them over the edge?

> ³His brothers therefore said to Him, "Depart from here and go into Judea, that Your disciples also may see the works that You are doing. ⁴For no one does anything in secret while he himself seeks to be known openly. If You do these things, show Yourself to the world." ⁵For even His brothers did not believe in Him (John 7:3-5).

At one point Jesus goes through his hometown and it says that he could do few miracles there because of their unbelief.

> ⁴But Jesus said to them, "A prophet is not without honor except in his own country,

among his own relatives, and in his own house." 5Now He could do no mighty work there, except that He laid His hands on a few sick people and healed *them*. 6And He marveled because of their unbelief. ... (Mark 6:4-6A)

It was more than their unbelief. It was their being unable to get past who they thought that he was. This stigma never left him. This scandal followed him until his death. In John, we see the Pharisees accuse his mother of adultery and Jesus of not knowing who his Father was.

41"You do the deeds of your father."

Then they said to Him, "We were not born of fornication; ..." (John 8:41A).

Jesus lived under this his entire life. What's more amazing is that he chose it. He went through thirty some odd years of life under this and never once did he have an ungodly or unrighteous thought towards any of these people. There was no sin in him. There was no bitterness. There was no anger. There was no retaliation. Only love.

These are the ones that he danced and whirled about over in Proverbs 8, as I talked about in chapter one. These are the ones that he would die for. Why did he do it? He wanted to give you victory as a human being over the arena of your heart. Before him, no man had been able to accomplish it before.

Someone accuses us and we get defensive. Someone slanders us and we grumble and complain and maybe even call him or her to the carpet on the matter. Someone gossips about us and we immediately call our spouse or best friend to vent about it. He did none of it. The only times in the gospels we see Jesus being defensive is on someone else's behalf.

He rebuked the Pharisees on behalf of the people, He defended the cripple on the Sabbath, he defended humanity from God's judgment of sin on the Cross, and he defended his mother in John 8, by calling her accusers sons of the devil.

44You are of *your* father the devil, ... (John 8:44A)

Everything he did, he did so you would be able to. Everything he did not do, he did not do it so you could resist. Every thought he took captive, he took captive so you would be able to. He lived life like everyone else, so that everyone else could encounter him in everyday life. He took on flesh so you could be filled with his spirit. He came in flesh, so he could be closer than your skin at all times.

What Now?

Is your Nazareth a coffee shop? Is it a cubicle? Is it an office? Is it a school? Is it home? Are you struggling to see where the dots connect from the past seasons of life? Are you just getting started and feel like you have the world at your fingertips? What is your story? What is your history in God?

Maybe it's time to look at your history again through His eyes, now that you know how he feels about you and how he sees your current position in life. It's time to rewrite your story, with God in it. Whatever your location or vocation is, the truth remains the same. It is your place of encounter.

Whether you mop floors, run a multibillion-dollar corporation, take a nap, or raise the dead, he will love you the same. He did not pay the price for your success. He doesn't need your success. He wants your heart. He wants your love. Your failures will never outweigh his love for you.

Your journey was designed for you and you alone. There is no one else that loves him the way that you do. You are the primary instrument he uses to establish his kingdom on the earth.

Napoleon Bonaparte, the great conqueror once said, "Alexander, Caesar, Charlemagne and I myself have founded great empires; but upon what did these creations of our genius depend? Upon force. Jesus alone founded His Empire upon love."

7

HOW FAR LOVE IS WILLING TO GO

As we close the book out, we must once again look at Christ. People in every field of life have been betrayed by a coworker, family member, or a friend. The great dilemma we face, and often fail, is not the betrayal itself, but how we respond to it. Betrayal is one of the most difficult situations to handle with Godliness.

Everything in our culture urges us to get even in some clever manner that will be painfully remembered. How do we carry our hearts in the midst of these moments? The answer is Christ. He is the only standard we have for loving others and loving God. How does God carry his heart when he is betrayed? The answer is found in Christ.

If we want to see what God is like, we must look at Jesus. If we want to see what humanity was designed to be like, we must again look at Jesus. I imagine that many reading this are already beginning to feel uncomfortable. Don't. Jesus will never command us to do something that he has not or is not willing to walk out himself. And, what he has walked out he has made available to you as well.

21When Jesus had said these things, He was troubled in spirit, and testified and said, "Most assuredly, I say to you, one of you will betray Me." 22Then the disciples looked at one another, perplexed about whom He spoke.

23Now there was leaning on Jesus' bosom one of His disciples, whom Jesus loved. 24Simon Peter therefore motioned to him to ask who it was of whom He spoke.

25Then, leaning back on Jesus' breast, he said to Him, "Lord, who is it?"

26Jesus answered, "It is he to whom I shall give a piece of bread when I have dipped *it*." And having dipped the bread, He gave *it* to Judas Iscariot, *the son* of Simon. 27Now after the piece of bread, Satan entered him. Then Jesus said to him, "What you do, do quickly." 28But no one at the table knew for what reason He said this to him. [29]For some thought, because Judas had the money box, that Jesus had said to him, "Buy *those things* we need for the feast," or that he should give something to the poor.

[30]Having received the piece of bread, he then went out immediately. And it was night (John 13:21-30).

This passage always left me scratching my head and dumbfounded by the disciple's reaction. They asked who the betrayer was, and Jesus not only told them, he showed them! How could they not see the answer so plainly given to their questions just moments before? Surely, if Peter had known what Judas was up to he would have never left that room. However, once we understand the cultural dynamics around this event, everything changes.

Scholar Will Barclay writes;

"When we understand aright what was happening, we can see that there was appeal after appeal to Judas. First, there were the seating arrangements at the table meal. The Jews did not sit at the table; they reclined. The table was a low, solid block, with couches around it. It was shaped like a U, and the place of the host was in the centre.

"They reclined on their left side, resting on the left elbow, this leaving the right hand free to deal with the food. Sitting in such a way, a man's head was literally in the breast of the person reclining on his left. Jesus would be sitting in the place of the host, at the centre of the single side of the low table. The disciple whom Jesus loved must have been sitting on his right, for as he leant on his elbow at the table, his head was in Jesus' breast... but it is the place of Judas that is of special interest.

"It is quite clear that Jesus could speak to him privately without the others overhearing. If that is so, there is only one place Judas could have been occupying. He must have been on Jesus' left, so that, just as John's head was in Jesus' breast, Jesus' head was in Judas'. The revealing thing is that the place on the left of the host was the place of highest honour, kept for the most intimate friend...but there is more.

"For the host to offer the guest a special titbit, a special morsel from the dish, was again a sign of special friendship. When Boaz wished to show how much he honored Ruth, he invited her to come and dip her morsel in the wine (Ruth 2:14)... When Jesus handed the morsel to Judas, again it was a mark of special affection. And we note that even when Jesus did this the disciples did not grasp the significance of his words. That surely shows that Jesus was so much in the

77

habit of doing this that it seemed nothing unusual. Judas had always been picked out for special affection."

Can you imagine Jesus and Judas walking into Passover that night to sit down? I can just hear Jesus saying, "Judas, why don't you sit to my left tonight? I'd love for you to sit there so we can talk." I wonder if Judas was able to keep his poise in the midst of it all. I wonder if he walked into dinner with a measure of resolve to do what he was about to do.

What always baffled me more than Judas' emotions was the response of the disciples. I used to think, "How could they be so dull?" But imagine, the sign to point out the betrayer is the sign of intimacy, honor, and friendship that Jesus showed Judas. No wonder the disciples were confused when Jesus handed him the bread.

Jesus wasn't having a mental lapse of memory during all of this either. He was not naïve to Judas' agenda or wicked desires. In John 17, Jesus expresses full mental recollection of eternity past and the glory he was clothed in before taking on flesh. After they left the garden, when Judas came to Jesus, Jesus called him friend. The Greek work is "*hetairos*." It means, "comrade" or "brother in arms."

In other words, Jesus looks Judas in the eye, as he is about to betray him, and says, "Judas, my friend, I would fight to the death for you." And indeed he did. This wasn't Jesus giving us an example of how to love those who betray us. This was Jesus loving a friend who was betraying him. Jesus' experiences as a man were not to set examples for us or for mere demonstrational purposes.

This wasn't God's version of show and tell. This is Jesus, the God-man, living life as a man. We cannot excuse one measure of his humanity here because of his divinity. Jesus was betrayed by a friend and he loved him to the end.

He is our standard. His commands sting when we hear them. "Love your enemies, bless those who curse you." We keep waiting for the transitional word that will get us off the hook like "however" or "but." But, they never seem to come. His commands are invitations into the vast arenas of His heart. We must never pass them up.

These commands require a context to work in, which means you will have enemies and you will have people who curse you. These are not the fun moments of life. However, it is only in this age that these moments are available. This is the only chance you get to respond to an enemy or bless someone who curses you. Once you go to be with the Lord in heaven, or he returns and establishes his kingdom on the earth, these opportunities to love like Christ will pass away.

These invitations only come in this lifetime. When we respond in love, it produces love in our hearts, and moves Christ's. When we respond in kindness, it produces kindness in our hearts. I don't mean to be wishy-washy and flippant, or muster up some measure of kindness in our flesh. It requires more strength to enter into love in the midst of hate than it takes to simply react out of anger. We must act and not react. It looks and sounds foolish. In many cases, it will look weak. Then again, so did the cross.

Every season of life yields an invitation to rediscover or discover anew the arenas of Christ's heart. Most invitations come at a cost. The invitation to love in the midst of betrayal will come at the cost of a betrayal. The invitation to love in the midst of pain will come through pain.

It's not about the situation. Rather, it's about the movements of his heart toward us, and ours towards him in the midst of it. The times we are betrayed give us access to know how Jesus' heart moved when he was betrayed, and these times allow us to love him for how he responded. Christ is more than our model for loving people, he is the way we love people.

My prayer for those who read this book is that you walk away with one simple, but profound goal: fall in love with Jesus Christ. He already loves you. Quit trying to earn it. You can prophesy, heal the sick, raise the dead, make millions, feed the poor, go to church, and even run a church, but without love, all of it is for nothing. You won't always have the sick, poor, or dead, but you will always have love. You will always have Jesus. Pursue him and may you love people in a way that produces worship. Amen.

Made in the USA
Las Vegas, NV
01 November 2021

33514844R00055